ME TO YOU

Discovering Joy in Selfless Love

SOULSHIFT
Bible Study

Connie Lightfoot

wesleyan publishing house
Indianapolis, Indiana

Published by Wesleyan Publishing House
Indianapolis, Indiana 46250
Printed in the United States of America
ISBN: 978-0-89827-477-6

Writer: Connie Lightfoot

This Bible study is a companion book to Steve DeNeff and David Drury's *SoulShift: The Measure of a Life Transformed* (Indianapolis, Ind.: Wesleyan Publishing House, 2011).

CONTENTS

INTRODUCTION

At College Wesleyan Church, a member went home after hearing a sermon on Me to You and tried to practice it. According to his wife, as he lay in bed one night, he turned to her and muttered, "I'm practicing Me to You, honey, so why don't you get up and turn out the lights?"

Many times I've preached a sermon and not known where it would land or how it might be used. Such stories spoken in jest (I hope!) only heighten my anxiety. I know that much depends on each person's interpretation and how he or she lives it out. How am I going to change? What am I going to do differently? That is the question, isn't it?

That is why I'm excited about the *SoulShift* study books designed to go deeper into each shift. This one, written by my friend and a member of our church, Dr. Connie Lightfoot, is an insightful, practical, crisply written piece with great stories that will help you turn big ideas into simple actions. Connie is the dean of professional and graduate studies at Taylor University. The stories in this book are ones only she could tell.

The shift from Me to You is perhaps the most primitive and fundamental of all seven. There is a reason we address it first in *SoulShift*: Many other shifts are possible once we have shifted from Me to You, but it is also one of the hardest to maintain. We are bombarded every day by media telling us, "You are the most important person in the world." "You are an army of one." "Have it your way." The number of books and articles devoted to self-esteem or self-help has more than doubled in the last thirty years. And accordingly, universities across the nation report record numbers of students who suffer from narcissistic personality disorder. Somewhere I read of a study comparing teenage diaries written in 1890 with those written in 1990, and the differences were startling. One hundred years ago, teenagers resolved to think before they spoke, work hard, have self-control, and invest in others more than themselves. Those from 1990 were quite different (remember, these kids would be in their thirties today). They resolved to lose weight and get new contacts, haircuts, makeup, clothes, and accessories. There is a definite shift in priority and focus.

Connie knows our generation, which may have invented the systematized focus on the "me" in our culture. She knows firsthand how all of us from every generation are naturally curved inward upon ourselves. God has given her tremendous insight into breaking this spell and freeing us, for the first time, to be genuinely more interested in others. Let her come alongside you and take you on a journey she has been on for years.

Steve DeNeff
Senior Pastor, College Wesleyan Church

HOW THIS STUDY WORKS

This four-week *SoulShift* study has two components. You'll do part of it alone and part of it together with a group of people in an existing small group, Bible study, or class. Each week includes five daily readings. You will want to encounter these with a Bible and pen in hand. Each reading has a Scripture reference so you can consider some aspect of moving from Me to You in the context of God's Word. Within the readings, you'll find questions to ponder. You might highlight them and take a moment to think about them right away. Or you can meditate on a question throughout the day.

There are also questions each week for your group to discuss together. Your discussion group may be new or have years of connection. Whatever it is like, use this *SoulShift* study to take things to the next level. Start by sharing from your heart on the issues raised and how you are being led to shift from Me to You.

The questions related to shifting your soul are many. We come into this world selfish by our very nature. All too often, we leave it the same way. But God is calling us to a shift in orientation from focusing on ourselves to focusing on others. This study can be another step in that journey.

WEEK 1

REACHING OUT

"Jesus sends us into the boardrooms where people haggle over power, into the families where the trust has been destroyed by broken promises, and into the boroughs of cities where people are wrapped up in their addictions. Jesus points toward the last vestiges of racism and unemployment, where men have been robbed of their dignity; to the nursing homes, where those who no longer seem useful to society are now marginalized; or to the hospitals, where patients sit quiet and afraid. He calls us to look into the hearts of such people and see the kingdom: What are their true needs? What help is still available to them? What is God's dream for them?"[1]

DAY 1

EPHESIANS 1:15–23

Paul had heard about the way the Ephesians loved all people (v. 15). If Paul were here today, what would he hear about your church or small group? What specific actions would lead someone today to comment about a group's love for all people?

Sometimes you have to receive grace to learn to give it. That happened for me after the doctor spoke the word none hope to hear: *cancer*. The journey to overcome breast cancer taught me much about moving from Me to You.

I was a first-year university academic dean. In the midst of hiring twenty-three faculty members, the to-do list never ended. A professor stopped by and said that he and his wife wanted to organize meals for us while I was getting radiation. I was touched and thanked them, but said that we had no need and that many others could benefit more from this kind gesture. A couple of days later, he sent an e-mail with the same offer. Then came more phone calls and e-mails. This guy wouldn't take no for an answer! He finally said, "Well, we're doing it, and you might as well tell us which nights you want food, because we already have the people lined up."

Finally relenting, I was surprised at the results of receiving this grace in my life. The nights those meals appeared at my office door were the exact nights when I could barely put one foot in front of another to get home. The meals were delicious and nutritious and paid special attention to my need for extra protein during radiation. I thought I didn't need help—but I did. The meals were truly a gift from loving people, some of whom I had never met, and reminded us each time of God's love for me and all of us.

YOUR SOULSHIFT

Have you shown love to a friend or relative recently? How about an acquaintance? What have you done that would visibly show the love of God to someone observing your actions? Can you do something today? Or at least plan something for later this week?

"For this reason, ever since I heard about your faith in the Lord Jesus and your love for all the saints, I have not stopped giving thanks for you, remembering you in my prayers."

—Ephesians 1:15–16

The life to which we are called in Ephesians spurs us on to action as we ponder the "incomparably great power for us who believe" (v. 19). We have the same power that raised Christ from the dead available to us. Tap into that power and do something you didn't imagine you had the strength or energy to accomplish. Write down what you plan to do so you have a reminder and are sure to follow through. Pray that God will direct your thoughts to the person who can most benefit from a visible reminder of God's love through your actions.

DAY 2

EPHESIANS 3:1–21

Do these verses awaken in you a longing to be "filled to the measure of all the fullness of God" (v. 19 TNIV)? What does it mean to have the fullness of God? Perhaps it's when your love leaks. By this I mean when God's love leaks out from you to others.

When babies nurse or drink from bottles, they lay back their head, completely content and entirely full. When this happens, they often smile and a little milk leaks back out of their mouth. Can you imagine being so full of God's joy that you leak a little of his love as you share his fullness in your life with others?

My eighty-something parents live on their own and do it quite well. Dad's dementia slows them down, but my problem-solving mother takes him out daily to provide continued stimulation. This keeps the walls from closing in and their world from shrinking.

During a long winter when yet another set of events had been cancelled due to the weather, my folks went to a restaurant where they enjoyed burgers and fries for lunch. They were sad about further cancellations but determined not to let it spoil the day. Their attentive waiter brought the bill while they were finishing. Just a few minutes later, the same waiter quietly retrieved the bill without comment. Thinking he had brought the wrong bill, Mom soon asked for the bill so she could complete the transaction. He informed them that a young fellow and his son who had been eating at a nearby table had paid the bill already. They were shocked. He hadn't greeted them or said a word, but he must have been watching.

> "Now to him who is able to do immeasurably more than all we ask or imagine, according to his power that is at work within us, to him be glory in the church and in Christ Jesus throughout all generations, for ever and ever! Amen.
>
> —Ephesians 3:20–21

Mom and Dad held their tears until they got out to the car but then sobbed their praise to God who lifted their spirits with the actions of a stranger. Did he recognize the vacant look in Dad's eyes? Did he notice how hard Mom was working to help Dad walk with his cane and get settled at a table? What moved him to provide this generous act? I have a guess. I think the fullness of God was leaking out of that young man.

YOUR SOULSHIFT

Who around you needs an unexpected act of kindness from a stranger today? Are there people God is placing in your path that you could help? Try to find one stranger you can assist today. Watch for places where you can show God's love.

DAY 3

EPHESIANS 2:11–22

The apostle Paul told us that we are "being built together to become a dwelling in which God lives by his Spirit" (v. 22 TNIV). I want to be the absolute best dwelling place for God's Spirit I can be. How can moving from Me to You accomplish this?

Sometimes there are unintended consequences we fail to see in moving from Me to You. I have a good friend (who I'll call Maria) in her late fifties who recently found her soul mate and will soon be married. Our university community reacted to this engagement and upcoming wedding with thrilled excitement.

As I pondered the changes in Maria's life, I thought of her best friend (whom I'll call Donna) who was also a single person in her fifties. How must Donna be feeling? Donna and Maria drove to church together each week nearly an hour away from their homes. What would it be like for Donna to drive alone to church? They shared a home for some time, shared many aspects of their lives with one another, and were still neighbors. Maria was not only moving to a new area, she was moving into an entirely new era of life. But what about Donna? She had to move into a new era as well but without the new benefits or positive changes Maria would have.

I debated how to reach out to Donna and even consulted Maria for advice. Maria was relieved that someone else was thinking of her friend and encouraged me to do whatever I could. I composed a carefully worded message expressing what I thought Donna might be feeling and saying that I was concerned about her and felt sorry for the changes she was experiencing. Donna immediately wrote back expressing her surprise that I had thought of her and said she was glad to be remembered.

"Don't you know that you yourselves are God's temple and that God's Spirit lives in you?"

—1 Corinthians 3:16

I resolved to have weekly lunches and invite her to dinner when our yard was in full bloom, knowing she and my husband share a love of horticulture. I can't take the place of Maria in Donna's life, but by expressing interest and following up with her, I hope I can aid in her transition and validate the emotions she will be experiencing.

Ephesians 2:19 reminds us that we are "fellow citizens with God's people and members of God's household." Giving that extra thought to unintended consequences is one way to show our love for others who are members of God's household.

YOUR SOULSHIFT

Who do you know who could use some extra, intentional connection from you? Are there circumstances at work that might cause your coworkers pain? Do you know of friends who are facing some unintended consequences in life? Would your acknowledgment of that pain assist them? If so, reach out. Don't wait; be bold. Your efforts could be rebuffed occasionally, but in my experience, people nearly always appreciate the thought. You can enrich someone's life simply by expressing concern and making a concrete offer to help.

DAY 4

EPHESIANS 2:1–10

What good works has God prepared you to do? Consider the strengths you have been given that can provide evidence of God's love to those around you. Who is equipping you for these tasks and how?

Sara was beautiful, bright, and blonde. She was frequently the only woman in my classes, which made her stand out even more. Sara knew every student in every class and made all of us laugh on a daily basis with her timely wit. We became good friends long before she left school. She graduated, found her first job, and married, and those were bittersweet moments for me. I missed my friend.

When Sara learned of my cancer diagnosis, she asked if she could stop in on a Sunday afternoon with her new husband. (Since she lived nearly three hours away, it was a pretty intentional drop-in.) Sara's laughing presence was like a tonic to me in my illness. Before leaving, she pulled out a large gift bag stuffed with small, wrapped packages. "These are little presents for you to open each day either before or after your radiation treatment," she said shyly as she handed me the bag. "I hope it helps cheer you up to have a present each day to counteract the reality of the radiation."

How had she found out exactly how many radiation treatments I had left? And how had she ever found so many little presents?

There were all kinds of gifts: candy, gum, earrings, stickers, markers, bookmarks, lipstick, nail polish, etc. There were more than thirty gifts in all. So many times I'd return to the car after a treatment feeling ill, and then like an expectant child, I would remember that I had a present to open. I cried as I opened some of those thoughtful little presents. To think that Sara cared enough about me to spend all of that time, money, and effort gave me strength and pointed me to our loving heavenly Father.

"What good is it, my brothers, if a man claims to have faith but has no deeds? Can such faith save him?"

—James 2:14

YOUR SOULSHIFT

Ephesians 2 reminds us that we are "created in Christ Jesus to do good works, which God prepared in advance for us to do" (v. 10 TNIV). What good works are on your list today? How can you concentrate on someone else and show in a visible way that you are thinking of him or her? Can you be a friend like Sara was to me for someone else this week? What creative talents or strengths do you have that God can use? Add to the list you started on day 1. What good can you accomplish this week? Start moving from Me to You.

DAY 5

EPHESIANS 4:1-13

Gentleness is a contagious trait. My husband is one of the gentlest people I have ever known, and I think his gentleness is rubbing off on me—because I wasn't gentle when we first met. We often worked with our daughters on gentleness as a trait they needed to acquire. One of the first verses we had them memorize was, "Let your gentleness be evident to all. The Lord is near" (Phil. 4:5 TNIV).

No one needs gentleness more than those who have lost a loved one. It's easier to simply ask vague questions or talk about the weather hoping that you are getting their minds off the recent death. But it doesn't work, does it? When experiencing grief and loss, the gentle word is the right word.

One gentle and well-timed word that works with those who have lost a loved one is to first think of the next holiday they will face without that person. For instance, if the friend lost a parent, Mother's Day or Father's Day will be particularly difficult. Then write a note, such as, "I realize this holiday will be difficult for you, and I'm thinking of you." This will be a gentle healing word. You can't take away the pain, but you can gently remind the person of God's love and care by remembering them and sending a note.

YOUR SOULSHIFT

Are gentle words a part of your life? Do you search for the right words to say in difficult circumstances? Can you think of someone who has lost a parent in the last six months? Would it be best for you to send a note right now so you don't forget? An unexpected, thoughtful gesture is one of the best ways to move from Me to You.

"A gentle answer turns away wrath, but a harsh word stirs up anger."
—Proverbs 15:1

GROUP DISCUSSION GUIDE

Another doctor wanted more tests to rule out yet another terror-inducing disease. My daughter Kendra was only five years old, but she had been sick for most of her life. It seemed never-ending.

The test was a sleep-deprived electrocardiogram. During prayer time, I asked my classes to pray about this test, especially since we had no idea how to keep a five-year-old awake all night. A couple of weeks later, a committee of students from those classes showed up at my office door to teach me an unforgettable lesson about Me to You.

The students wanted to entertain Kendra through the entire night. They had prepared a schedule where Kendra would visit with students who had each planned thirty minutes of activities for her. We were to relinquish Kendra at 9 p.m. and pick her up at 6 a.m. I was stunned, and a little scared. However, we knew a night of fun and games would be better than my husband and me trying to entertain her while falling asleep ourselves.

With a significant amount of nervousness, I dropped Kendra off on that Tuesday evening with the first student. That night, she would bake cookies, slide across a bubble-lined floor, play games, make crafts, color, and have a great time. When I picked her up the next morning, she was dirty, on an incredible sugar high, full of stories, and giggling about all the stunts they had pulled.

We never did learn exactly what caused Kendra years of serious illness, but she is a healthy mother and college professor today. I saw Jesus at work that morning as I pulled away from the university. Students who had been willing to crawl out of their beds at 4 a.m. to play with a five-year-old they didn't know spoke to me louder than a hundred sermons. Those young students knew what it meant to practice Me to You.

As a group, create a list of instances when the unexpected attention and care from someone vividly reminded you of the One we serve. What examples can you find? Spend the next few minutes making a list of when you have seen the hand of God through the actions of others. How can you take similar action? Who has God placed in your path that you could shower with kindness and thoughtfulness and help him or her see Jesus?

LEADER TIPS

Hopefully the first week of the study will excite your group and get them thinking about others in a new way. Try to get started right by checking on their progress with the questions each day. Are they simply reading the lesson, or reading and doing? If you encourage the group to share ways they are trying to live out these passages and concepts, they will get ideas from one another and begin the long process of learning how to carefully hold one another accountable.

QUESTIONS

Here are the passages that were used in this week's readings. Turn to each passage together and highlight the verse or idea that is most important to you.

- Ephesians 1:15–23
- Ephesians 3:1–21

- Ephesians 2:11–22
- Ephesians 2:1–10
- Ephesians 4:1–13

1. Of these passages, which one might God be leading this group to consider more deeply, and why do you think so?
2. Which of the above Ephesians passages gave you a nudge to stop thinking and start doing? Write out that verse and put it on your bathroom mirror to remind you to continue moving from Me to You this coming week.
3. Share with the group what ways you tend to be a thinker rather than a doer.
4. With your lists and notes from the week, compare yours with others. Make a list on a large piece of paper of all the ideas from each set of questions for the week.
5. Start a list for your group of concrete methods of moving from Me to You. Group the items mentioned into general categories that might help the group to generate additional ideas.
6. What commitment will the group make for action in the upcoming week? Consider sharing a gentle act of kindness that God seems to be leading each of you to do for a stranger. Return next week with stories to tell.

As a group, pray for each other's concerns and specific ways God is offering opportunities to move from Me to You.

WEEK 2

CROSSING BOUNDARIES

"When the soul shifts its tracks toward God, each churn of the wheels delivers more freedom. You're moving farther from sin and death. The person born selfish . . . becomes selfless. It's a shift in the soul that can only be possible by Christ's sacrifice. You're right—it's not natural; it's supernatural."[2]

DAY 1

EPHESIANS 4:17-28

I sometimes shy away from new experiences. I know the people living in nursing homes are just regular people who have needs. But a young woman (who I'll call Gloria) taught me a lesson that took years to take hold in my stubborn heart.

Gloria was the wife of a computer science major and was a few years older than most of my students. Gloria had a sweet spirit and was others-focused. My husband and I hired her to care for our daughters while I taught. She was a wonderful caregiver and played with our girls constantly. One day, Gloria asked if she could take our daughters to the local nursing home with her. I asked why, and she responded that she had a couple of friends she wanted to visit. Never one to pry, I didn't question her further.

That night the girls were so excited to tell me about the pictures they colored to give Gloria's friends. I soon learned that Gloria visited the nursing home after she moved to town and asked which residents rarely received visitors. She made friends with three or four of those residents and regularly visited. Gloria and her husband were struggling to make ends meet during his college years, but she gave what she had—her time. I ended up visiting Gloria's friends with her, but I was still uncomfortable with the surroundings and never went back. I watched Gloria live out Me to You, yet I did not participate.

Over thirty years later, the tables were turned. My mother-in-law had to enter a nursing home, and I remembered Gloria and her friends. I did everything I could to make my terminally ill mother-in-law comfortable, from washing her hair to convincing our children and grandchildren to visit. But I still carefully gave space to the other residents and hurried to and from her room. I pushed away Gloria's example of Me to You and excused myself because I was busy and needed to assist my mother-in-law.

"Therefore, as God's chosen people, holy and dearly loved, clothe yourselves with compassion, kindness, humility, gentleness and patience."

—Colossians 3:12

Now, five years later, we've signed my dad into a nursing home. His dementia is worsening and Mom can no longer care for him. But this time, with a nudge from my memories of Gloria's compassion for others and thoughts of Me to You, I have walked more slowly through the halls, stopping to visit with other residents. I have looked into their eyes and exchanged conversations with them. I am not fearful or uncomfortable as I move toward Dad's room. I am hopeful that a new attitude is taking hold in my heart.

Gloria's lesson took a long time to learn—too long. But I think I am getting there. Me to You. Three very short words, only seven letters. But they can be a very long journey.

YOUR SOULSHIFT

How has God been speaking to your heart about a situation where you could make a difference? Are there people who you struggle to see as people God loves? How could you grow in this area? What groups of people are hard for you to love? What new attitude is God developing in you?

DAY 2

EPHESIANS 4:29—5:2

Lessons from my daughters are not easily learned. When I was in my thirties and forties, I developed a storytelling technique that was effective in groups and the classroom. I learned I could hold the attention of a group by carefully unfolding the details of a story. The laughs when I hit the punch line were worth the effort of crafting the story with thought. A good story needs some outlandish moments, so I learned to embellish to get the effect I wanted. I don't know exactly when it happened, but my stories were sometimes based on good story elements more than on facts. I started with a real event, but embellishing made for a better story.

Our youngest daughter was in high school when she began to point out inaccuracies in my stories. I usually laughed it off or somehow made her look silly, but it bothered me. I tried to talk to her about storytelling and how it was important to craft a story. She would say, "That isn't true. That's Mom embellishing the story again." That cut deep.

However, I began to realize that she was right and I was wrong. I was not "building others up . . . [to] benefit those who listen" (v. 29). I was twisting the truth to make myself look good as I told the story.

This habit had crept into other verbal parts of my life. Half-truths didn't bother me if they made an impact or my point effective. Once I became aware (thanks to my daughter's correction) of my inaccuracies or lies, I repented and began building a new habit of speech. I can still tell a story to get a laugh from a group or class, but now my words are true and not embellished. (After all, life is usually funny enough without embellishment!) I believe that my soul was shifting as I learned to make my words "benefit those who listen."

"Do not let any unwholesome talk come out of your mouths, but only what is helpful for building others up according to their needs, that it may benefit those who listen."

—Ephesians 4:29 TNIV

YOUR SOULSHIFT

Are your words trustworthy? If not, can you identify a few instances where you enhanced the truth to get a particular effect? Now can you repent for those times? Do you need to correct misstatements in your past with people you know? This takes great concern for others and less for yourself as you seek to benefit others—embellishments only benefit you.

DAY 3

EPHESIANS 5:3-16

There are people in my life who seem to naturally think of others rather than themselves—as though they were born with it. But no one is born with it. I am beginning to think they are simply further along in the Me to You transition; maybe they've grown more than me in that area.

The woman I spoke of before, Gloria, is married to Daniel (also not his real name), an intense, Vietnam veteran who lived a rough life before he found Jesus. Raised by a single mother in the inner city of Miami, Daniel was imprisoned for armed robbery after he left the armed forces. Drugs had been a part of his life, and they left him diabetic and with other health concerns. Although he never complained, Daniel probably didn't feel well most of the time. Lying on his cot in prison and reading the Bible over and over, Daniel found Jesus. Daniel knew his Bible as well as any layperson I know.

Given his difficult background and relatively new faith, I would expect Daniel and Gloria to pick a strong church with many options for Bible study and growth. But they didn't. They found a small, struggling, inner-city church that couldn't even afford a preacher every Sunday. They built relationships with the (mostly elderly) people and began to minister the love of Jesus to them.

They were devoted to the small church and used their own gifts to assist with the church.

When Daniel found a job in Pennsylvania, they lived in the suburbs but attended church in the inner city. We went to visit them and weren't even sure our car would be safe during the morning worship service. The people in that inner-city location loved Daniel and Gloria. They had a powerful ministry there and spoke often to our hearts about the comforts of our lives. They eventually sold that little house in the suburbs and moved into a row house in the city to increase their potential impact. Daniel and Gloria live and breathe a Me to You life, and it's a great example to me.

"But if we walk in the light, as he is in the light, we have fellowship with one another, and the blood of Jesus, his Son, purifies us from all sin."
—1 John 1:7

Ephesians 5 encourages us to flee the darkness and walk as "children of light" (v. 8 TNIV). I believe that Daniel and Gloria learned how to share the light of Jesus in very dark places and to do it with a loving heart. Shining the light of Christ in a dark place is one way to shift your soul toward others.

YOUR SOULSHIFT

Does your church have a ministry in difficult places such as an inner-city context? Are you drawn to serve in that way? Should you be more drawn that way? You might not think it fits you, but putting the interests and needs of others before yourself and your own comfort is the key.

DAY 4

EPHESIANS 6:1–3

Gloria came from a strong Mennonite family in western Pennsylvania. Her parents (who I'll call Jim and Nan) were great examples of Me to You to their family. They raised their four children to always look for ways to give . . . and they did. Their oldest son had a powerful ministry in several small towns in Maine near the end of the Appalachian Trail. The churches were too small to support a full-time pastor so he pastored them all at once. It wasn't an easy life for him or his family, but it was a calling, and he worked at it with all his might.

After a round of influenza, he was struck by Guillain-Barré syndrome resulting in paralysis. Hospitalized for months, he regained only slight usage of his hands and was paralyzed from the waist down. Jim and Nan were semiretired and deeply involved in a variety of ministries. But without a second's thought, they packed up their lives in Pennsylvania and moved to Maine to care for the children and keep the household going during their son's extended illness.

Parental love is an amazing thing, but love of this magnitude shows us Me to You. Jim and Nan never acknowledged or discussed their sacrifice. They were simply thankful they were unencumbered and able to assist their son and his family. What would you do for your children (or other family member) if needed? We often say we would do anything for our children, but some people don't when the time comes. It's only those who have moved along in selflessness that are ready when the crisis hits.

YOUR SOULSHIFT

"'Honor your father and mother'—which is the first commandment with a promise—'that it may go well with you and that you may enjoy long life on the earth.'"

—Ephesians 6:2–3

Most of us don't need to minister directly to our children in this way, but is God asking it of us for others? Is he preparing us for bigger sacrifices in our future by asking for smaller ones now? There are people all around us with immense needs. How is God leading you to assist? If not yet with your parents or children, then who?

DAY 5

EPHESIANS 6:4

If you have children, do you pray daily for their spouses or future spouses? Selecting a mate is one of the most significant decisions we watch our children make. After assisting them with decisions through their entire lives, it isn't easy to leave this one in their hands. Is this yet another instance of Me to You?

Jim and Nan are my favorite success story of moving from Me to You as their only daughter, Gloria, made her unflinching choice of a spouse. Of conservative Mennonite descent, Gloria did two years of volunteer service before going to college. Choosing a small, Christian, two-year college, she soon met Daniel, who was enjoying his release from incarceration and new life in Christ. God was always at the center of their relationship, but you can imagine the reaction when Gloria brought Daniel home for the first time.

Jim and Nan had carefully prepared to launch their four children into adulthood. One had already died when the ultralight plane he was piloting crashed before their eyes and killed him. Although they were protective of their daughter, they wanted her to live her own life and find God's call. However, they never expected Gloria to bring home a former drug user who had served time in prison for criminal activity. But that's who Gloria brought home to her parents.

Jim and Nan carefully began exploring who this young man was and how he had won their daughter's heart. Over time, they embraced his differences and loved him. They even took him around in their conservative Christian community and asked for acceptance for their daughter and her beloved.

"'For I know the plans I have for you,' declares the LORD, 'plans to prosper you and not to harm you, plans to give you hope and a future.'"
—Jeremiah 29:11

When I met Jim and Nan, they were still getting used to their new son-in-law and enlisted my help (as I was his professor and advisor). They wanted to know how to give him the help he needed to succeed. The light in his eyes, placed there by the joy of knowing Jesus, was wonderful to behold, but Daniel had to learn to look people in the eye and confidently shake their hands. He was smart, but the schoolwork of a liberal arts institution required a great deal of work on his part. He quickly proved himself on all fronts, however, and showed all of us how the grace of God could truly transform a person.

Jim and Nan love their son-in-law and are thankful for the now more than twenty-five years of Gloria and Daniel's marriage. Their four children are delightful and further evidence of God's grace. Jim and Nan learned Me to You in a special way as they welcomed Daniel into their family. They realized that God had purposes for Gloria's life that were very different than what they had envisioned, yet it was in the will of God for their daughter.

YOUR SOULSHIFT

In what ways do you need to trust God today for your children or others for whom you're concerned? Allowing God's purposes for others is not always easy, especially when it involves those we love, but it may be the most important Me to You step we can take.

GROUP DISCUSSION GUIDE

We've spent this week looking at parts of Ephesians 4–6. Start your group meeting by reading these short chapters aloud, perhaps with each person reading a paragraph. Sometimes I feel like Ephesians contains enough challenges for me for the rest of my life. There are so many practical lessons and wonderful advice. Our souls would truly shift if we could live out the material in Ephesians. Ask each person to point out a verse or concept that resonated with them this week.

Me to You has many different angles. During this week, we have tried to explore some of the more obscure or difficult ways to experience this SoulShift. It is likely that one or more of the stories in the last week will spawn further examples from the group. Take time to explore those and see what further principles you can extract. Or maybe your group needs a field trip to a nursing home or rehab center. Are there others (like me) who have avoided such experiences like the plague?

LEADER TIPS

Could your group provide some interest or respite from the monotony for the inhabitants of a nearby nursing home?

Whatever your group decides, be sure there is a concrete plan to exercise their newfound understanding of Me to You. The new attitude discussed in Ephesians 4:23 ought to find an outlet in action resulting in steps toward Me to You.

QUESTIONS

Here are the passages that were used in this week's readings. Turn to each passage together and highlight the verse or idea that is most important to you.

- Ephesians 4:17–28
- Ephesians 4:29—5:2
- Ephesians 5:3–16
- Ephesians 6:1–3
- Ephesians 6:4

1. What questions did the daily readings generate in the group?
2. Were the Me to You aspects of parenting important for you to hear? Share with the group what ways parenting is a key part of shifting from Me to You. Spend a few minutes sharing about the children in group members' lives and even praying for them and their spiritual lives. For those in the group who do not have children, discuss how you can do selfless things for younger people who are not your biological children, but in some ways are your spiritual children.
3. Discuss with the group a time when a parent did something very selfless for you.

Take time as a group to pray now for your concerns and ongoing shift from Me to You.

WEEK 3

SHOWING LOVE

"That is what it is all about for those who have moved from Me to You. The heart of the shifted soul is broken by the needs of others, not the self. The eyes of the shifted soul are constantly looking to the needs of others, not the self. What's Me to You about? In one word: *others*."[3]

DAY 1

PHILIPPIANS 1:9-11

As dean of a Christian university, I have often used today's passage as a prayer. On a daily basis, my work calls for knowledge and depth of insight. And to "discern what is best and may be pure and blameless for the day of Christ" (v. 10 TNIV) is frequently needed as I move through a usual day of problem solving. I remember some of the first lessons I learned in showing the love of Christ and struggling to find a depth of insight.

The year was 1972, and I was in the spring semester of my freshman year of college. A first course in computer programming sparked a huge interest in me, and I was enthusiastically learning how to utilize the room-sized computer that managed the university business and served as a tool for every student taking computer courses. Our labs were always in the evening, because the computer was used for university business during the day.

"Whoever loves his brother lives in the light, and there is nothing in him to make him stumble."
—1 John 2:10

The head of the fledging computer department hired a graduate of the business program who had also picked up some computing skills. His name was Jere Truex, and I had no idea I was meeting a person who would be my dear friend and mentor for many years to come. Jere was a quadriplegic. After a bout with polio when he was seven years old (the polio vaccine was discovered just a year later), his body never grew and became more and more misshapen.

To prevent it from curling, he had his spine fused, making it impossible for him to ever occupy a chair. He lived on a small stretcher that could be loaded into his specially equipped station wagon. He slept in an iron lung and used a respirator during the day. Jere had just enough movement in his right hand to get the long metal pipe of the respirator into and out of his mouth for each breath. His skill at computing was considerable, although small compared to the brightness of his magnetic personality.

His friendly, cheerful, and funny way made him a delight as a lab assistant. And that was true even to this eighteen-year-old, sheltered, freshman girl who had never been around a person who was truly disabled.

Jere frequently showed his intellect as we held our computer listings in front of his face; he would quickly suggest what we were doing wrong. He was brilliant, even graduating summa cum laude. But more important than his intelligence was his zest for living and focus on others. Jere truly enjoyed his hours of helping hapless freshmen learn a bit about computer science. And we learned to appreciate his depth of insight and vibrant outlook on life. I think I took a tiny first step toward Me to You during those weeks of learning to know the remarkable Jere Truex, someone who could have been very self-focused but never was.

YOUR SOULSHIFT

Is there someone who has a physical or mental handicap in your sphere of influence? How can you befriend him or her? Moving from Me to You is a journey of tiny steps. Why not take a step by seeking out a new friend? In what ways and environments do you feel at a disadvantage in your life? How can you be selfless in those contexts?

DAY 2

PHILIPPIANS 2:1-4

How do you react when you meet a person with significant disabilities? I tried to return Jere's smiles and wit, although I was sometimes struck dumb by the reality of his limitations. Jere used humor to show us effortlessly how to assist him. As a lab assistant, he was often mouthy and funny in a borderline inappropriate way. One evening when his behavior was particularly bad, I took courage in hand and rolled his stretcher into a closet and shut the door. I made sure his respirator was still plugged in but we could hear him laughing and shouting at us for the few minutes we left him in there. I asked him if he was ready to behave when he emerged and he meekly promised to "keep it clean."

"Dear children, let us not love with words or tongue but with actions and in truth."
—1 John 3:18

Jere always had a new joke or story to make us laugh, and it wasn't long before all of the students were eager to spend time with Jere as a lab assistant. When Jere attended a sporting event and wanted to taunt the opponents, with his slightly mobile right hand he would hold up a sign which read, "I could do better than that!"

Years later, my husband and I took Jere to a nice restaurant where the service staff took great care of us. We usually tried to go at off times to make it easier to trundle the stretcher and respirator into the restaurant. This time, the restaurant had been empty when we arrived but filled as we lingered over our dinner.

Jere nearly always ordered a huge hamburger and ate it in three or four bites while my husband fed him. I tried to make him eat vegetables, but he always claimed he was helping out mothers everywhere by not eating them. Why? He wanted us to point to him and tell our children, "That's what will happen if you don't eat your vegetables!"

As we threaded our way through the suddenly quiet, crowded restaurant, a quick-witted man who knew how to relate to people with disabilities said loudly, "The food can't possibly be *that* bad in here!" Jere howled with laughter and retold the story over and over again.

Humor is an amazing gift, and I'm convinced that it can assist us as we learn how to relate to people with disabilities. What better way to show Me to You than to gently spar, when appropriate, with him or her? We are often told that those with disabilities prefer not to be treated differently than others. Kidding around and finding humor in awkward situations is, I believe, an excellent way to do that.

Today's passage says, "In humility value others above yourselves, not looking to your own interests but each of you to the interests of the others" (vv. 3–4 TNIV). How better to do that than to reach out to a person with disabilities?

YOUR SOULSHIFT

Who has God placed in your path? Is there someone who needs an extra smile, joke, or story? How could you spend some meaningful time with a person who has no way to experience activities or events without assistance? Relax, be comfortable, and try building a relationship with someone who is different. It will likely move you further along in your journey from Me to You.

DAY 3

PHILIPPIANS 2:19–24

Philippians 2:21 says, "For everyone looks out for their own interests, not those of Jesus Christ" (TNIV). While Paul was describing what is generally true of most people, it can become less true for us as we move from Me to You. As we consciously look out for the interests of others and that reaction becomes more natural, we begin looking out for the interests of Jesus Christ instead of our own.

"Dear friends, let us love one another, for love comes from God. Everyone who loves had been born of God and knows God."
—1 John 4:7

Jere taught me a lot about not looking out for my own interests. During the 1980s, I lived in Muncie, Indiana, and only saw Jere on a sporadic basis until he decided to get a masters degree at Ball State University (BSU) in Muncie. For the first time, Jere was going to live in a residence hall (along with his full-time caregiver) and attend classes in person instead of listening to them over the phone. It was a daunting challenge, but BSU prided itself on being an accessible campus, and they were willing to give it a try.

Jere loved his year at BSU. Trundling across campus on his stretcher in all sorts of weather was a completely new experience. His good nature and sense of humor carried him through some of the situations needing patience. He excelled in his coursework and managed to attend every class.

He hit some roadblocks, though. At home, he had a computer terminal with a detachable keyboard, and he could use a stick with his slightly mobile right hand to poke keyboard keys. He was deadly accurate and amazingly quick with it. However, BSU had no way to get a terminal with a separate keyboard for him, and we couldn't move his keyboard to Muncie.

He hesitantly asked if I would come to the residence hall and type as he talked so he could get his programs entered into the computer. Jere needed someone who understood computer programming and could type quickly as he spoke.

I was a young mom, teaching part-time, with a preschooler and a nursing baby at home. Our budget was tiny and childcare wasn't an option for us. Paul and I struggled with the decision but ultimately realized that giving time to Jere was an investment we couldn't ignore. I believe we moved several steps along the Me to You continuum as we found times when Paul could watch the girls so I could drive to campus to type for Jere for a couple of hours.

Thinking of others is not a natural state for us—even as believers. Yet I believe Jesus would have gladly gone to that residence hall to type for Jere, and I was pleased to do so as well. It was a small inconvenience for a short amount of time that produced growth in us. Doing what was right was worth the time and effort.

YOUR SOULSHIFT

When is the last time you inconvenienced yourself for someone else? Can you do it again this week? There is no better use of our time than looking out for the interests of Jesus Christ. Consider how you might build more margin in your life so you have some time to serve others.

DAY 4

COLOSSIANS 3:12-17

Today's passage says to "clothe yourselves with compassion, kindness, humility, gentleness and patience" (v. 12 TNIV). All these qualities make for good Me to You "clothing," but compassion may be the first thing to wear in becoming selfless.

One of my pet peeves is when someone insists on always pointing out the positive when there is a problem. You know the type. Mechanical difficulties make me miss my flight and disrupt my travel plans. Instead of sympathy, this person will say, "Oh well, at least you got home!" That statement is true, of course, but my heart longs for compassion and a touch of sympathy. "Man, that must have been tough at the end of a long trip to not get home when you expected. So frustrating!" A reaction like that makes me look at the positive and I might be likely to follow up with a response such as: "But at least I made it home."

"Be kind and compassionate to one another, forgiving each other, just as in Christ God forgave you."
—Ephesians 4:32

Jere was a master at compassion. Someone with the massive challenges he faced could either become resentful and sour or incredibly compassionate. He could become bitter or better. I'm thankful that Jere chose compassion instead of bitterness.

I remember a time when I had a really rough day at work. I was a mid-level administrator, and Jere lived about four blocks from my office building. I left the office to walk off the anger and frustration and found my steps heading, quickly and angrily, to Jere's house. I flew in the door and burst into tears. I felt foolish as I looked at my friend who couldn't even move his limbs yet I was complaining to him! But Jere extended that withered, misshapen arm and comforted me as I sobbed out the story and cried on his shoulder.

I felt better as I slowly walked back to work and the situation that awaited me. But I think I felt better partly because of the contrast between what Jere had and what he offered me. His life was incredibly difficult and yet he could, without a single incriminating word or look, comfort me compassionately in my hour of need. If I ever react with compassion, it is partly because God showed me compassion at a moment when I needed it through a man with a withered, nearly paralyzed arm.

YOUR SOULSHIFT

How do you react to the difficulties of others? Have you found a way to show compassion without making others feel guilty for complaining, condemning their shortsightedness, or trying to solve every problem too quickly? A person with this kind of compassion has moved from Me to You.

DAY 5

COLOSSIANS 4:2–6

Colossians 4:6 says, "Let your conversation be always full of grace, seasoned with salt, so that you may know how to answer everyone" (TNIV). What does this verse teach us about mentors and mentoring?

Who has mentored you? Having been a female dean at two different Christian universities, I am often asked that question when being interviewed. For several years, I responded that I really had no personal mentors but simply a long series of excellent teachers who made me want to be like them.

"But as for you, continue in what you have learned and have become convinced of, because you know those from whom you learned it."
—2 Timothy 3:14

But when telling my career path to yet another eager group of graduate students a month ago, I realized that Jere had played the role of mentor to me. He was always proud of me. In fact, he was directly responsible for my first full-time teaching position.

When I was about four months pregnant with our third child, my good friend and still chair of the computer science department of my alma mater, called to ask whether I would teach a course during the spring semester. Despite learning that I would be giving birth around finals week, he persisted, insisting that we could finish early or someone could help near the end of the semester. As a way to get off the phone, I finally said that if Jere Truex would agree to teach the course with me, I would do so.

To my total shock, Jere agreed. He was nervous but wanted to use that brand new graduate degree he had earned to do something, so we were suddenly a professional team. Can you imagine the look on those young students' faces when we rolled Jere in on four wheels with a respirator clenched in his only hand that moved? And I was so pregnant that I erased the bottom half of the chalkboard while writing on the top. The students were good sports about it, and we had a great semester that finished with me grading papers while my third daughter snoozed in her crib in my hospital room.

After that exercise in 1981, Jere went on a campaign for me to take a full-time teaching position. He was relentless. When a position opened up at our alma mater, he nearly filled out the application for me. I was offered that teaching position, and Jere was with me for the next several moves as I changed from teaching to administration to a doctoral program and back to teaching. He was always my cheerleader and supporter.

I have tried to pass this trait along by encouraging younger professionals. I try to speak into their lives by verbalizing strengths I see them exhibiting. I often suggest they look at the next level and prepare themselves. I try to fill my conversations with grace, always sprinkled with salt, to encourage and motivate the people God places in my path.

YOUR SOULSHIFT

Are you an encourager by nature? Who are you specifically encouraging or mentoring right now? If there aren't at least five names on your list, how about selecting some and getting started on this part of the quest of moving from Me to You?

GROUP DISCUSSION GUIDE

The exploration of Me to You this week has centered on people with disabilities and how to approach relationships with them as part of our efforts to move from Me to You. It is probably obvious that Jere Truex had a large effect on my life. Next to my grandparents, his death has been the one I grieved most. However, it is also a joy to think of Jere as physically whole again, able to walk and run and fully move his arms! But his absence here was a huge loss for me personally.

One thing was clear when talking to people at Jere's funeral: Many of us felt like we knew him better than anyone else did. I was pretty sure that he was my friend and others were merely his acquaintances. I was wrong, of course. Jere had an uncanny ability to devote himself so fully to you as an individual that you truly felt that he couldn't possibly focus so intently on someone else.

I'll never forget my last encounter with Jere. I knew he had been sick with a bad cold, that can be deadly to someone who can't cough, sneeze, or even breathe on his own. It had been a slow recovery, and he was willing to admit that he didn't feel good. I stopped by to see him on a Friday night just to tell him I missed him and see how he was doing. There were other people at his house, but somehow, he and I went off by ourselves and had a very meaningful conversation. We quickly became serious, and I told him how he had influenced me on a couple of recent decisions and thanked him for his wisdom and friendship. We told one another that we loved each other, and I left feeling like we had really connected. The next morning, he told his mother good morning, and when she returned with his breakfast, he was gone. His big heart just stopped beating.

LEADER TIPS

I hope that as your group discusses any thoughts from this week that you can explore the impact a variety of people have made on your group. Who has shown them compassion? Mentored them? Taught them to look outside of themselves?

How can you and your group pass on those lessons to others? Who can you befriend, show compassion to, mentor, or assist with life's needs?

If there are people in your group who have never connected to a person with disabilities, encourage them to find ways to do so. All of you will be richer for stepping out into this unfamiliar territory as you move from Me to You.

QUESTIONS

Here are the passages that were used in this week's readings. Turn to each passage together and highlight the verse or idea that is most important to you.

- Philippians 1:9–11
- Philippians 2:1–4
- Philippians 2:19–24
- Colossians 3:12–17
- Colossians 4:2–6

1. As a group, divide into pairs (preferably not married couples) and share with the other person all of the people you know (and see on a somewhat regular basis) who have disabilities. Even if you don't know their names, talk about them. Discuss what you've done or could be doing to be selfless around these people. What are you learning from them?
2. As a large group, recall the times in which Jesus encountered disabled people. If you can remember the Scripture passages, cite them for others to write down. Jesus did heal, but he often did more than that. What actions did he take beyond healing? What words did he use? How does this provide an example to emulate?
3. Again meet in pairs with the same person from before. Share now who the people are in your life that aren't physically disabled but in some ways are limited by emotional or psychological stresses and dysfunctions so that interacting with them is very difficult. (You don't have to share names.) Discuss what you've done or could be doing to be selfless around these people. What are you learning from them?

Spend some time in prayer with your group partner instead of praying with the larger group. Pray for each other's concerns and also for ways in which you can both selflessly serve some people in difficult situations, and that God would continue to shift you both from Me to You.

WEEK 4

CORRECTING SIN

"It has been said that the final test of any religion is how it affects our relationships with other people. Our relationships serve as mirrors for the soul; they show us how spiritual we really are."[4]

DAY 1

1 PETER 1:17–25

For this last week of our study, I would like to highlight another application of the concept of Me to You that may not be obvious. As an educator, I have had to deal with academic dishonesty and cheating on many occasions. It is never easy to handle. I have never fully understood why, but when a student cheats, it feels like a personal affront.

> "Now that you have purified yourselves by obeying the truth so that you have sincere love for each other, love one another deeply, from the heart."
>
> —1 Peter 1:22 TNIV

Once the discovery is made that cheating has taken place, confrontation must occur. After the confrontation, punishment must be planned and given. Students who have readily confessed may feel that they shouldn't have to pay for their behavior. Those who deny the charge will inevitably be angered by a punishment. Sometimes these situations are appealed to a higher level which can mean a lot of time and effort for all parties. The cycle can be long and difficult.

When the student is repentant, the situation is much easier to resolve. I have gone through this point a few times and found that my relationship with the student can be healed and even stronger. Students with a sensitive spirit and willingness to listen to authority often are grateful for a second chance at relationship despite the punishment.

This is where Me to You comes into play. It would be very easy to withhold approval or act differently toward students who have failed to be honest. But after years of dealing with these unfortunate situations, both as a professor and as an administrator, I believe that restoration of the relationship is key in assisting the student to grow in character and spirituality. If I am concentrating on me and how I feel about the situation, I am unlikely to be considerate of the embarrassment, shame, or other negative emotions the student is likely feeling. If I can put myself in his or her place and think of how I would like to be treated after a moral failure, I am much more likely to react with compassion.

Love is what we need to show to people who have been dishonest. We need to have courageous conversations with them. If you have a friend who is living an ungodly lifestyle, what is your responsibility? Can you obey the truth and sincerely love by confronting that friend with truth? Is this difficult responsibility part of shifting from Me to You? I believe it is an important part that requires great effort.

YOUR SOULSHIFT

Are there some courageous conversations you need to have soon? Can you bathe the situation in prayer and outline a plan of how to confront your brother or sister in love? What truth can you speak that will assist him or her to realize that he or she is living outside the will of God? Are there inequalities or difficulties you have chosen to ignore rather than confront?

Moving from Me to You permeates many aspects of our lives and asks us to do uncomfortable things. Are you willing to do the hard things? What has God put on your heart that needs to be lovingly confronted?

DAY 2

1 PETER 2:1-3

At the end of a graduate hooding ceremony the night before graduation, I received a call from the registrar indicating discovery of a graduating senior (who I'll call Melanie) who had forged the names of four faculty members on a form needed for graduation. The form was late, and she had been repeatedly informed that the paperwork was not in order for her to graduate. At nearly 5 p.m. on that Friday, Melanie brought the needed form into the office. When processing it, the eagle-eyed employees noticed that the signatures were not the usual ones. A few phone calls later, they knew they had a forgery. They called Melanie and left urgent messages for her to return the call. But by 9 p.m., they had heard nothing.

"Therefore, rid yourselves of all malice and all deceit, hypocrisy, envy, and slander of every kind."
—1 Peter 2:1 TNIV

I suggested they continue calling and inform Melanie that I would need to meet with her prior to the graduation ceremony. The registrar's office, her advisor, and the head of the department repeatedly tried to contact her to no avail.

About ninety minutes before graduation, I got the call that they had found her in the line for graduation. Overnight I had discussed the situation with the provost and the dean of student development.

We all agreed that the reasonable and fitting punishment was that she could not participate in the commencement ceremony. But we had expected to inform her prior to the start of it.

Not knowing how she (or her family) would react, the campus police were called and other officials were nervously hovering nearby while the registrar and I (wearing full academic regalia) confronted her with our findings. At first she denied it, but she soon realized we had confirmation from the four faculty members. She confessed and immediately began apologizing and suggesting she would properly fill out the form on Monday morning.

She was horrified when I indicated that she would not be allowed to participate in commencement. Melanie truly believed that she would be allowed to participate if she were simply sorry enough. But I couldn't relent. There were few punishments possible at the eleventh hour and this dishonesty, which actually broke the law, was not something we could overlook.

Sometimes Me to You means looking into the future and determining what action or punishment has the greater likelihood of getting the attention of a believer not growing in Christlikeness. We all need accountability to rid ourselves of evil traits. We need to be willing to assist fellow believers in moving forward to be like Christ.

YOUR SOULSHIFT

Do you have situations where you need to compose yourself to do the hard thing? Do you err on the side of relenting in difficult situations when you ought not? Think through your current situations and make certain you are carrying through with correct reactions and accountability. Remember that moving from Me to You involves accountability.

DAY 3

1 PETER 2:11-25

Once Melanie was convinced that I was serious and that she wouldn't be allowed to participate in the ceremony, I suggested she call her parents to tell them. Her dad did not answer his cell phone.

Once we found them (or rather they found us) in the arena, I motioned for Melanie's parents to follow me. On the way to a quiet corner of the vestibule, many questions ran through my mind: How would they react? Would they be furious with me? The institution? Their daughter? Would they insist on speaking with someone higher up? While Melanie fumbled through the horrid story, I was fervently praying for the right words and reactions.

> "Submit yourselves for the Lord's sake to every human authority."
> —1 Peter 2:13 TNIV

Their reaction merits a "parents of the year" award, in my opinion. They were angry and sad, as you would expect. But their immediate reaction was that the institution was doing the only thing it could, and they were very disappointed in their daughter. They still loved her and would stand beside her as we resolved this unfortunate situation.

After fifteen minutes of reeling and absorbing this news, her father said, "Well, I came to attend a graduation and by gum, we're going to attend a graduation. You are sitting with us through the entire ceremony." What an unexpected answer! My respect for Melanie's parents immediately rose. They were charting their path by setting aside the tremendous emotion and thinking what would be best for their daughter. Seeing her name in the printed program but not hearing it read would be a bittersweet moment, but Melanie's parents made huge strides that day in moving from Me to You.

From my place on the stage, I tried in vain to spot them during the ceremony. My thoughts and prayers were with them during the entire celebration. But one fortunate young woman was learning the lesson of a lifetime from parents who knew what she needed. I can only imagine the anger they felt. I am fairly certain that they wanted to convince us to allow her to participate in commencement, but they immediately submitted themselves to the decision of the university and complied without argument. It was an amazing display of faith in action.

YOUR SOULSHIFT

What about you? How do you react when unexpected and uncontrollable events happen? Can you think clearly and respond as Jesus would? Is your immediate reaction one that concentrates on the other person rather than you? This reaction, without rehearsal, is one of the telling indicators of your movement from Me to You.

DAY 4

1 PETER 3:8–12

I tried to contact Melanie several times, but there was no answer until about six weeks later. We received a request from Melanie for a meeting with the campus pastor, her advisor, the registrar's office, and me. We found out that Melanie's dishonesty about her school work went back years to community college courses that she never passed. She had only recently been completely honest with her parents (and herself). God convicted Melanie who gradually admitted all of the lies to her parents. You can imagine their shock and outrage.

Melanie desperately wanted forgiveness from us. Her parents had forgiven her although their emotions were still very raw. After hearing the entire tale of woe, we each told her we were sad about the dishonesty, forgave her, and longed to see her finish her degree. After a time of prayer together, we all rolled up our sleeves and put together multiple scenarios of how she could complete her degree at our university or by transferring courses.

"Be like-minded, be sympathetic, love one another, be compassionate and humble. Do not repay evil with evil or insult with insult."

—1 Peter 3:8–9 TNIV

We didn't get all of the details settled that day, but we left that room nearly three hours later rejoicing in forgiveness and restoration.

I believe Melanie learned a lot about moving from Me to You during that encounter. She learned the reality of forgiveness. She learned that a bunch of college administrators can be pretty creative in their solutions to such a maze of details. She could see the tears on our faces and the understanding in our eyes. Melanie stood tall as we all shook hands at the end of the lengthy meeting. The reality of forgiveness and the ability to think of the other person made all the difference in Melanie's life that day.

The people Melanie met had no desire to do her evil. Our thoughts (without conversing) were like-minded. We all wanted to assist Melanie in her quest for forgiveness and restoration. The Spirit was very near to us that day. We all had the sense that we were part of a much larger picture than what the work day often brought.

YOUR SOULSHIFT

How do you react when confronted with your inadequacies? Are you angry, hurt, embarrassed, or defensive? Do you immediately think of the person who is confronting you and how difficult this is for that person? Can you take the next step of Me to You to think of others when you are hurting or angry? Think back over a couple of situations where you've been confronted and rescript it with a Me to You ending. Can you live that out when the next confrontation occurs? What if the shoe is on the other foot? If someone confesses sin to you, can you listen, offer forgiveness, and then immediately begin the restoration process? Me to You moves us to think of the other and react in his or her best interest instead of our own.

DAY 5

1 PETER 4:7–11

To my total surprise, Melanie, with her parents' encouragement and blessing, chose to return to our institution to repeat her senior year and meet the requirements she had failed to complete. Not only did we get her registered in the needed courses, but we also set up a gauntlet of supports. Melanie had to promise to meet regularly with a counselor, an advisor, the academic support center, a pastor, and me. This was all to help Melanie stay on track and deal with her issues of deception.

> "Above all, love each other deeply, because love covers over a multitude of sins."
> —1 Peter 4:8 TNIV

It was a daunting schedule for Melanie, but she accepted our plan. Her parents were pleased with our efforts, and we became a team to assist Melanie. We all wanted her to succeed in her school work and graduate but, more importantly, we wanted her to become Christlike and learn the importance of always dealing in truth.

Melanie completed each requirement I asked of her. Her grades were good and I started noting a spring in her step, directness in her eye contact, and a sparkle in her eyes. She was getting it. By the end of the yearlong process, I was regarding Melanie and her parents as friends. I looked forward to our meetings to hear of Melanie's progress. I met with her folks when they came to campus, and we compared notes on Melanie's progress. I could ask her direct questions like, "Have you been untruthful with anyone in the last week?" and be reasonably sure that Melanie was telling me the truth. The grace of God can make a wonderful transformation in a person.

In this instance, an entire team of people was practicing Me to You. Without thought of the amount of time we were giving to one individual when there were many, we each responded to the challenge of creating an environment where Melanie could thrive. She may not have always enjoyed the process, but I know Melanie felt cared for as we lavished her with attention and accountability.

YOUR SOULSHIFT

Me to You is not always easy. It sometimes requires a massive investment of time and talent. Are you willing? Can you be the accountability person for someone who needs it? Can you force yourself to ask the hard questions and confront the possibilities when it would be easier to keep the conversation light? Is there someone God is placing on your heart right now who could benefit from your investment as you move from Me to You?

GROUP DISCUSSION GUIDE

There is, of course, a happy ending to the story. Melanie completed those two semesters of requirements and chose, with her parents, to participate in graduation. We all saw graduation as the fitting end to the horrid events of graduation day a year earlier.

It had been a costly year. The family paid for an additional year of private college. Melanie endured a year with a rigorous schedule allowing little time for fun or downtime. Her parents had calloused knees from their hours of prayer for their daughter and those who were working with her. But realizing that Melanie had earned a degree she was now proud of was worth all of it. Knowing that Melanie was walking in the light instead of the darkness was worth any price. Reveling in a job well done was gratifying for all involved.

There aren't enough hours in the day to be involved at this level with many people. But the personal satisfaction and growth that comes from seeing firsthand what the grace of God can accomplish helped each of us in our quest to move from Me to You. We may have been doing our jobs, but the intensity and success made this an especially rewarding venture. Is there joy in moving from Me to You? Yes. Few things give more joy than moving our focus from the self to others.

LEADER TIPS

Summarizing this month of lessons should be the objective during your final meeting. The first week dealt primarily with lighter or easier ways to move from Me to You. Week 2 challenged us to think of how to interact with the less fortunate people we sometimes avoid. Week 3 explored the idea of reaching out to people with handicaps and improving our willingness to interact and enrich their lives as well as our own. And we finished with discussions of sin and evil and how to courageously confront those situations in the name of Jesus.

Survey the group to see which category of lessons moved them to action. Is there a plan to work on at least one aspect of moving from Me to You? Encourage each individual or couple to make concrete plans to take action.

QUESTIONS

Here are the passages that were used in this week's readings. Turn to each passage together and highlight the verse or idea that is most important to you.

- 1 Peter 1:17–25
- 1 Peter 2:1–3
- 1 Peter 2:11–25
- 1 Peter 3:8–12
- 1 Peter 4:7–11

1. What are moments in Scripture where you see people keeping others accountable, confronting them for their actions, or admonishing them? How can we speak the truth in love in these ways?

2. Why do you find it hard to resolve conflict or confront another person's actions? In what ways is this in fact a move from Me to You? Do you get much out of confronting someone, or is there almost always more risk than reward?
3. Can you name a time when someone confronted you about something you really needed to hear? Are you now thankful for that person? Were you at the time? Share with the group how you've changed because of the confrontation.
4. Is there accountability needed within your small group? Suggest some mechanisms to continue to discuss the concept of moving from Me to You. How can you create a structure for measuring continued progress?

Take time to pray as a group, perhaps even standing and holding hands, asking God to make you a selfless people for years to come.

“God’s dream for you is to dream for them more than yourself—to act in such a way that their needs are met before your own, to be so selfless as to help before you hoard. He wants you to entertain others rather than yourself, to move from Me to You. Why? Your love for God is no greater than your love for others.”[5]

NOTES

1. Steve DeNeff and David Drury, *SoulShift: The Measure of a Life Transformed* (Indianapolis, Ind.: Wesleyan Publishing House, 2011), 39–40.

2. Ibid., 37.

3. Ibid., 38–39.

4. Ibid., 39.

5. Ibid., 40.